ReadingWise

Comprehension Strategies That Work

4

Series Consultant

Diane J. Sawyer, Ph.D.
Murfree Professor of Dyslexic Studies
Middle Tennessee State University

ReadingWise 4: Comprehension Strategies That Work
ISBN 1-56420-328-X
Copyright © 2003 New Readers Press
New Readers Press
U.S. Publishing Division of Laubach Literacy
1320 Jamesville Avenue, Syracuse, New York 13210

Printed in the United States of America
9 8 7 6 5 4 3 2 1

All proceeds from the sale of New Readers Press materials
support literacy programs in the United States and worldwide.

Developer: Kraft & Kraft, New York, NY
Series Editor: Judi Lauber
Production Director: Heather Witt
Designer: Shelagh Clancy
Illustrations: Alexander Jones, Matt Terry, Linda Tiff, Andrea Woodbury
Production Specialist: Alexander Jones
Cover Design: Kimbrly Koennecke

Contents

To the Student

Welcome to *ReadingWise 4*. This book will help you understand and remember more of what you read.

Good readers think when they read. This book is about the thinking skills they use.

Life has already taught you a wide range of thinking skills. This book will show you how to use them for reading.

ReadingWise 4 has 31 lessons. Each lesson builds one skill and has four parts:

- This Is the Idea tells what skill you will learn.
- Take a Closer Look shows how to use the skill.
- Try It helps you use the skill.
- Use It lets you use the skill on your own.

Adults need to read many things every day. This book includes

- news and sports reports
- opinion columns
- charts and graphs
- ads
- rules and directions
- how-to tips
- tables of contents
- texts in history, science, nature, and language
- and other things

As you read these things, *ReadingWise* helps you practice thinking skills. And the skills help you become a better reader.

Using Clues to Meaning

A writer may define or explain a word in the text. A writer might also use a *synonym*, another word that means almost the same thing. A word that you know can help you understand one that you don't know.

This Is the Idea

Read this part of a recipe and decide what *zest* is.

Making Orange Muffins

Mix the flour, sugar, and baking powder. Add the grated orange peel. This orange zest gives the muffins their special flavor. Set the mixture aside. Next, beat the eggs, milk, and oil. Pour this mixture into the bowl with the grated orange zest and the other dry ingredients.

What does the word *zest* mean here? If you look for clues, you will notice that the writer uses *zest* and *peel* in the same way. You can guess that *zest* and *peel* have almost the same meaning.

Take a Closer Look

Read this part of a how-to article and decide what *mastic* is.

What to look for
- Mastic is glue.
- mastic, which is glue
- mastic, or glue,
- the mastic, the glue,
- the mastic— the glue—

Getting the Tiles Down

Some flooring tiles have a sticky backing. You just press these onto the floor and roll them with a heavy roller. Other tiles require mastic, or glue, to stay in place. You can buy this mastic at most hardware stores. You apply the mastic to the back of each tile to stick it in place. Place the tile and then press it down with the roller.

Circle your answers.

1. What is mastic?
   a. tile   b. glue

2. What does mastic do?
   a. keeps tiles in place   b. rolls over tiles

Try It

Read this travel tip and decide what caverns are.

The Luray Caverns

Leave time to visit Luray Caverns, one of the state's famous tourist sites. Once you get inside the caverns, you will see why they are so popular. The caverns, or caves, form an underground maze of rooms. Some rooms are more than 100 feet tall, with very colorful walls.

Luray Caverns
Luray, VA

Circle your answers.

1. What is this travel tip about?
   a. Luray Caverns   b. tourist sites

2. What are caverns?
   a. walls   b. caves

Use It

As you read, decide what an article and an amendment are.

Articles and Amendments

The U.S. Constitution was quite short at first. It contained only seven articles, or main parts. Soon after the states accepted it, 10 changes—amendments—were made. Others came later, but the first 10 amendments are called the Bill of Rights. Those changes made certain rights clear.

Circle your answers.

1. What is this text about?
   a. articles and amendments   b. the first seven articles

2. What is an article?
   a. a change   b. a main part

3. What is an amendment?
   a. a change   b. a main part

4. What is the Bill of Rights?
   a. seven articles   b. 10 amendments

Getting the Picture

◆ *Understanding Figurative Meanings*

Writers often use words to create images. Sometimes the words say one thing but really mean something else. (If you're "climbing the walls," you're upset, but you're not really crawling up the walls.) Words used this way are called *figures of speech*.

This Is the Idea

As you read this news report, look for words that don't mean what they say. Look for figures of speech.

Mayor to Retire

RIVER CITY — In his retirement speech, Mayor Gomez said, "Being a mayor is like riding a roller coaster. Well, my ride is over now, and I'm a little out of breath. I want to thank everyone who worked so hard for this city. The mayor may be the quarterback, but it's the team that wins the game."

Is being a mayor like riding a roller coaster? It could be thrilling and scary. It could have its ups and downs. The mayor wasn't playing football, but his staff was like a team, and he led them the way a quarterback would.

To understand figures of speech

- If simple meanings don't make sense, think about what *would* make sense.

Take a Closer Look

As you read this ad, look for figures of speech—words that don't mean what they say.

River City Travel Vacation Specials

You can't stand the rat race any more because you've got so much to do that it makes your head spin. You're exhausted. Well, one of our vacation packages is the perfect way to relax and recharge your batteries.

Circle the meaning of *recharge your batteries*. **Hint:** Try each choice in place of *recharge your batteries* in the ad.

a. get your batteries ready to use in gadgets
b. get back the feeling of being full of energy
c. feel tired and worn out

Try It

As you read this advice, look for figures of speech.

Starting a New Job

Starting a new job can be upsetting. At first, being in a new setting with people you don't know may make you feel like a fish out of water. Try to build bridges to other people. A smile and a warm greeting can help break the ice.

Circle your answers.

1. How would "a fish out of water" feel?
   a. relaxed and comfortable
   b. upset and uncomfortable

2. What does it probably mean to "build bridges to other people"?
   a. get to know people
   b. leave people alone

Use It

As you read this news report, look for figures of speech.

Brock Sworn In as Mayor

RIVER CITY — Shasta Brock was sworn in as mayor today. In her remarks, she said, "This city has been down a rough road since we lost two major employers. But if we work together, we can turn River City around. I will focus on our schools, because knowledge is the key that unlocks the door of economic success."

Circle your answers.

1. When Mayor Brock said the city "has been down a rough road" she probably meant
   a. many people were out of work in the city.
   b. there were plenty of jobs for everybody in the city.

2. What did Mayor Brock mean by "turn River City around"?
   a. get the people all facing in a different direction
   b. turn from hard times in the city to good times

3. How is knowledge like "the key that unlocks the door of economic success"?
   a. People with knowledge are more likely to succeed.
   b. People who finish school get keys to the school doors.

Deciding How You'll Read

◆ *Predicting Content; Setting a Purpose and Method*

**Before you start to read, think about what you are going to read.
First decide why you will read.
One reason is to learn something.
Another is to find a fact quickly.
When you know why you will read, decide how you will read.**

This Is the Idea

Decide why and how you would read this newspaper listing page.

Sometimes you read to get just the information you need. What is this page about? It's about things to see and do around town. You aren't likely to read the whole page slowly and try to remember everything. You are likely to read it quickly to find the time for a movie or other event.

What to do

- Picture what you will read about.
- To learn something new, read slowly.
- To find a fact, read quickly.
- To help yourself remember, take notes.

Take a Closer Look

Decide why and how you would read the rest of this news report.

Heat Wave Bakes City

RIVER CITY — Seven straight days of record high temperatures have the city reeling. Forecasters say that a storm may bring relief in a few days. Meanwhile, older people are urged to avoid hard work if they can. You'll find tips for staying cool later in this report.

You might read the report quickly to find out when the storm may come. Circle a reason for reading it slowly and carefully.

a. to find out when the heat wave started

b. to find today's forecast

c. to find out how to stay cool during the heat wave

Try It

Decide why and how you would read the rest of this sports feature.

The Over-the-Hill Soccer League

River City's newest soccer league isn't for everyone. It *is* for everyone over 50. "There are lots of men and women in River City who would like to play soccer," says league founder Leah Ozer. "Some feel that they're too old. Our message is that you're never too old, so please join us."

Circle your answers.

1. Why would someone read the sports feature quickly?
   a. to learn more about some of the players in the league
   b. to find out how to join the league

2. Why would someone read the feature slowly and carefully?
   a. to learn the whole story of how the league got started
   b. to find when the next game will be played

Use It

Decide why and how you would read chapters in this book.

Contents

Chapter 1. Basic Facts about the Mississippi River.................

Chapter 2. How the Mississippi River Formed ....

Chapter 3. Shipping on the Mississippi River ....

Chapter 4. Wildlife along the Mississippi River ....

Chapter 5. The Future of the Mississippi River ....

T H E
MIGHTY
MISSISSIPPI

Circle your answers.

1. Why would you read Chapter 1 quickly?
   a. to find out how long the Mississippi River is
   b. to enjoy stories, legends, and tales about the Mississippi River

2. Why would you read Chapter 2 slowly and carefully?
   a. to find out whether the Mississippi River flows through Ohio
   b. to understand how the Mississippi River became so long

Asking the Right Questions

Asking questions helps you understand what you read. Asking questions helps you identify the most important parts of the text.

This Is the Idea

As you read these instructions, ask "Why?"

Are You Having Phone Problems?

Before you call the phone company, find out where the problem lies. It might be in the company's lines or in your phones. (Part 2, below, gives hints on how you can tell.) A repair call is free if the problem is in the company's lines. The phone company will charge you if the problem is in your phones or inside wires.

Why should you find out where the problem lies? Look for *where the problem lies* in the text. Right after that, you learn that the problem might be in the company's lines or in your phones. After *that,* you learn that a repair call is free if the problem is in the company's lines.

Take a Closer Look

As you read this biography, ask "Who? What? Why?"

Ask
- Who?
- What?
- When?
- Where?
- How?
- Why?

Wilma Rudolph's Amazing Feat

In 1960, Wilma Rudolph did an amazing thing. She won three gold medals for running at the Olympic Games. Rudolph had been disabled as a child. She wore braces on her legs until she was 11, but she wanted to be an athlete. She worked hard to reach her goal.

Circle your answers.

1. What did Wilma Rudolph do at the Olympic Games?
   a. won three gold medals   b. wore braces on her legs
2. Why was Rudolph's feat so amazing?
   a. She wanted to be an athlete.   b. She had been disabled.

Try It

Read this advice for people seeking jobs. Ask questions about it.

The Job Interview

A job interview gives you a chance to make a good impression. Be on time or a little early. You'll show that you're reliable and eager. Be prepared to answer questions. Be well groomed, and dress appropriately for the job that you want. Be polite, and show that you're interested.

PERSONNEL

Circle your answers.

1. Why should you be on time?
   a. to show that you are reliable   b. to be prepared

2. How should you be dressed?
   a. for the job you have now   b. for the job you want

Use It

Read this school memo to parents. Ask questions about it.

• BUS PASSES

Bus passes may be picked up at the principal's office. Each student will be assigned to one bus and given a pass to board that bus. Students cannot switch buses without a new pass. There are two kinds of passes—regular and day. A regular pass lasts for the entire school year. A child who needs a ride on a certain day may get a day pass, but only if space is available.

Circle your answers.

1. Where can you or your child get a bus pass?
   a. at the principal's office   b. on the bus

2. Why would your child need a bus pass?
   a. to get onto a bus   b. to get into school

3. What would your child need to switch buses?
   a. a note from you   b. a new pass

4. Why might your child not be able to get a day pass?
   a. The bus might be empty.   b. The bus might be full.

Checking as You Read

Monitoring Comprehension

Use a chart to check your understanding as you read.
First, decide what you already know about the subject.
Then decide what else you want to know about it.
As you read, keep track of what you learn.

This Is the Idea

Read the title of this brochure and look at the picture. What will the brochure be about?

You can tell that this brochure will be about federal income tax forms. What do you already know about tax forms? What do you want to find out about them?

Take a Closer Look

Keisha made this chart about tax forms. Read the information on it.

What I Already Know	What I Want to Know	What I Learned
Taxpayers fill out tax forms.	The kinds of 1040 forms	
The main one is form 1040.	How the forms are different	
There are different 1040s.	Which form I have to fill out	

1. Copy one thing that Keisha already knows about tax forms.

   _____

2. Copy one thing that Keisha wants to know about tax forms.

   _____

Try It

Look at this chart about tax forms, and decide what should go on it.

What I Already Know	What I Want to Know	What I Learned

1. Let's say that you already know this about tax forms. Put it on the chart.

   Form 1040EZ is the shortest and simplest.

2. Let's say that you want to know this about tax forms. Put it on the chart.

   Which form is the longest?

3. Add something else that you already know about tax forms.

4. Add something else that you want to know about tax forms.

Use It

Now read this part of the brochure to learn more about tax forms. What new facts do you learn?

Most taxpayers use Form 1040, Form 1040EZ, or Form 1040A. Form 1040 is the longest. The EZ version is the shortest and simplest. The A version is also short, but not as simple. Many people can use the shorter forms. However, you must file the long form if any of the following things are true for you:
(1) Your income is above a certain amount (Check the instructions.);
(2) You work for yourself;
(3) You have farm or rental income;
(4) You have money in foreign banks.

Add the things you learned to the chart above.

Putting It in a Few Words

As you read, pause now and then to think about what you've read. Sum it up by putting it into a few words. Those few words will be easier to remember.

This Is the Idea

How would you put this job tip into a few words?

After the Interview

After a job interview, many people just sit back and relax. They think there is nothing left for them to do. If you really want a job, though, keep working at it. Write a short note to the person who interviewed you. Thank the person, and mention that you really want the job.

You could sum up the important information in these few words: "If you want the job, send a note after the interview and say so."

Take a Closer Look

To sum it up

- Put the most important parts into a few words.
- Don't include details that aren't very important.

Read this part of an instruction sheet and sum it up in your mind.

THE HOT BUTTONS

This telephone has two red "Hot Buttons." These let you dial a call with one touch. The Hot Buttons save time during an emergency. To make other calls, you have to press more buttons. You can program Hot Buttons to dial your family doctor, a hospital, or a Poison Control Center.

What is the most important information? Check two sentences that you would use to sum up the answer.

_____ a. This telephone has two red "Hot Buttons."

_____ b. The Hot Buttons save time during an emergency.

_____ c. To make other calls, you have to press more buttons.

Try It

Read this parenting tip and think about how to sum it up.

Make Car Time Family Time

Many families spend a lot of time in cars. Some people see this time as wasted, but it does not have to be. Time in a car can be a good time to talk without interruption. Don't waste it by riding in silence or just listening to music. Instead, enjoy the chance to share the day's news.

Here are three ways that readers might sum up "Car Time Is Family Time." Circle the best one.

a. Families spend a lot of time in cars. Most people ride in silence or listen to music.

b. You can talk in a car without interruption. You can also ride in silence or listen to music.

c. Families spend a lot of time in cars. They should use this time to share the day's news.

Use It

Read this biography and think about how you would sum it up.

www.comstock.com

George Crum

Most people do not recognize George Crum's name. They do know his creation, though. Crum was a cook in Saratoga Springs, New York. In 1853, he tried cooking potatoes in a new way. First, he sliced them very thin. Then he dropped the slices into hot fat. We call his invention potato chips.

Circle the sentence that best sums up "George Crum."

a. People don't recognize the name George Crum.

b. In 1853, George Crum was a cook in Saratoga Springs, New York.

c. George Crum invented potato chips in 1853.

d. Potato chips are slices of potato cooked in hot fat.

Putting It in Other Words

◆ *Paraphrasing*

As you read, think about what the writer says. Think about other ways to say it. Putting ideas in other words will help you understand them. It will help you recall them, too.

This Is the Idea

How would you put this tax tip into other words?

> ## Keeping Good Tax Records
>
> When it comes to keeping tax records, neatness does count.
> The rule to follow is "When in doubt, don't throw it out."
> Keep every pay stub and canceled check. Keep every receipt
> for the things you buy. Keep a record of the expenses you pay.

You could put the rule to follow in these other words: "Keep every piece of paper, even if it doesn't seem important."

Take a Closer Look

To put it in other words

- Think about what it means.
- Look away from the text.
- Imagine telling someone what it says.

Read this part of a life story. Put the ideas in other words.

> ## The Inventor of the Modern World
>
> Thomas Edison invented or improved many of the gadgets that
> keep our homes humming today. He made the first phonograph.
> That led to the record player and CD player. He made the first
> practical electric light. His inventions helped develop early movies.
> He also worked to make better batteries.

Circle the sentence that puts the text in blue ink into other words.

a. Thomas Edison invented or improved many of the gadgets that keep our homes humming today.

b. Thomas Edison built or worked on many things that we use every day.

Try It

Read this part of a history article. Put the ideas in other words.

How Cities Grew

If you look at a map, you will see that most cities are on or near water. A source of water was one of the first things people looked for when they chose a place to settle. Many of the largest cities grew where trade routes crossed, and that often meant trade by water.

Here are two ways that readers might put the last sentence in "How Cities Grew" into other words. Circle the better one.

a. Because people like to live near water, many cities began near beaches and coves.

b. Because people shipped goods by water, many cities began near good harbors for shipping.

Use It

Read this nature article. Put the ideas in other words.

THE WATER WIZARD OF THE DESERT
◆ ◆ ◆

Saguaro cactus are well suited to life in deserts. They are good at getting water and keeping it. To collect as much water as possible, saguaro cactus have roots that extend a long way in every direction. To retain water, saguaro cactus have thick stems full of spongy pulp.

Getty images

1. Circle the sentence that tells about the roots in other words.
   a. Saguaro cactus have roots that reach far and wide to get any water that there might be.
   b. Saguaro cactus have roots that extend a long way in every direction to collect as much water as possible.

2. Circle the sentence that tells about the stems in other words.
   a. The inside of a saguaro cactus stem holds water the way a sponge does.
   b. Saguaro cactus have thick stems full of spongy pulp to retain water.

Deciding What It's About

◆ Recognizing the Topic

**Most news reports are about one topic.
Most charts, ads, and articles are about one topic.
Sometimes the topic is spelled out for you.
At other times, you will have to figure out the topic.**

This Is the Idea

Look at these catalogs and decide what they are about.

For the catalog on the left, the title and pictures work together. They help you decide that the topic is children's clothes. The title of the catalog on the right tells you that it's about something for the home. It doesn't tell you enough, though. The picture helps you decide that it's about furniture.

Take a Closer Look

How can you spot the topic? Look at

- a title
- a picture
- a headline or headings
- repeated words on one topic

Read this portion of a chart and decide what it is about.

Team	Won	Lost
1. Bisons	8	3
2. Rams	7	4
3. Bulldogs	5	6
4. Ravens	4	7

Circle your answers.

1. How can you tell what sport this is about?
   a. from the picture   b. from the names of the teams

2. Which title would fit this chart?
   a. Football Standings   b. Schedule of Games

Try It

Read this paragraph from an instruction book. Decide what it is about.

Removing the Wheel

Before you jack up the car, pry off the wheel cover. Then loosen the nuts on the wheel. Do not remove them yet. Now jack up the car until the wheel is about two inches above the ground. Finish taking off the nuts, and place them in the wheel cover so you don't lose them.

Circle your answers.

1. Which of these is mentioned in the title?
   a. the wheel   b. the jack

2. Which of these is shown in the picture?
   a. only the jack   b. the jack and the wheel

3. Which of these is the topic of the paragraph?
   a. how to use a jack   b. how to remove a wheel

Use It

Read this part of a history article and decide what it is about.

Clocks of Ancient Times

The oldest clock is the sun. People noticed where the sun was in its progress across the sky and judged how much of the day remained. To keep track of time at night, they made marks on candles and checked them as they burned or put sand in an hourglass and checked it as it flowed downward.

Circle your answers.

1. Which of these is pictured *and* is in the title?
   a. a modern clock   b. an old clock

2. Which of these is described in the paragraph?
   a. modern clocks   b. old clocks

3. Which of these better describes the topic of the paragraph?
   a. the latest clocks   b. the oldest clocks

Using the Topic

◆ *Anchoring Understanding on the Topic*

**First, decide what the topic is. (See Lesson 8.)
Then keep the topic in mind as you read.
Focus your attention on what is important to the topic.**

This Is the Idea

Which parts are important to the topic of this fabric care sheet?

————— **How to Wash Your New Sweater** —————

You're sure to enjoy the warm softness of your new sweater. Wash this sweater by hand in cold water. Dissolve soap in water and then drop the sweater into the soapy water. Let it soak for five minutes. Then rinse and dry flat. For a free catalog of our sweaters call 1-800-555-5555.

The title says that the care sheet will tell you how to wash your new sweater. The parts in blue ink explain how to do this. The parts in black ink are not important to that topic.

Take a Closer Look

As you read, ask yourself

- Is this about the topic?
- Is this really important to the topic, or just interesting?

Which parts of this article are most important to the topic?

The First Teddy Bears

Kids love teddy bears. Teddy bears were named for President Theodore Roosevelt. "Teddy" Roosevelt loved hunting. Still, he once refused to shoot a bear cub. An artist drew a picture of this. A store owner saw the picture and got an idea. He began making stuffed bears called "Teddy Bears."

Check the two statements that are most important to the topic. *Hint:* The topic is "the first teddy bears."

_____ a. Kids love teddy bears.

_____ b. Teddy bears were named for President Theodore Roosevelt.

_____ c. A store owner saw the picture and got an idea.

Try It

Which parts of this travel book are most important to the topic?

Buses in Mexico

Mexico has hundreds of bus lines. You can take a bus almost anywhere. Buses are not as widely used in the U.S. More people in the U.S. travel by car than by bus. Buses in Mexico can be plain or fancy. Some offer extras such as films and snacks. Trains are also a good way to get around.

Check two statements that are important to the topic of buses in Mexico.

_____ a. Mexico has hundreds of bus lines.

_____ b. Buses are not as widely used in the U.S.

_____ c. More people in the U.S. travel by car than by bus.

_____ d. Buses in Mexico can be plain or fancy.

Use It

Which parts of this sign are most important to the topic?

Wildlife Warning

Many people thrill at the sight of a wolf or fox. Enjoy looking at them, but never touch them. Keeping wild creatures as pets is against the law in most places. Wild animals may bite or scratch, and they can carry disease. Be sure to explain this warning to your children.

Circle your answers.

1. What is the sign about?
   a. keeping raccoons as pets
   b. looking for wildlife
   c. avoiding dangers of disease from wildlife

2. Which sentence is most important to the topic?
   a. Many people thrill at the sight of a wolf or fox.
   b. Wild animals may bite or scratch, and they can carry disease.
   c. Keeping wild creatures as pets is against the law in most places.

Finding the Writer's Point

◆ *Recognizing the Main Idea*

Writers sometimes state the point of the writing in a sentence. Sometimes they don't state it. Even if a writer does not state the point, you can often figure it out.

This Is the Idea

Read this part of a life story. Look for the writer's point.

Elizabeth Blackwell

Before 1849, no woman had become a doctor in the U.S. In that year, though, Elizabeth Blackwell got her medical degree. Many people at the time did not want women doctors. In time, more women followed Blackwell's lead. Soon, women doctors were more common.

You learn that no woman in the U.S. was a doctor before Elizabeth Blackwell. The writer could have stated the point of the writing as "Elizabeth Blackwell was the first woman doctor in the U.S."

Take a Closer Look

Read this feature article. Look for the writer's main point.

═══ Creating Depth in Pictures ═══

An artist might paint one tree overlapping another. Then the overlapping one will seem to be closer. The artist could also make one tree large and bright and the other small and pale. The large, bright one will seem to be closer.

To find the writer's point

- Look in the first or last sentence.
- Read all the sentences and decide what the writer wants to say about the topic.

Circle your answers.

1. What is this article about? *Hint:* Read the title.
   a. making paintings seem deep
   b. making trees seem large

2. Which sentence states the writer's point?
   a. When we look at a painting, some trees seem closer than others.
   b. Artists have ways of making flat paintings seem to have depth.

Try It

As you read this consumer tip, look for the writer's point.

Free Computer Time

Many people don't own computers yet want to learn about the online world. You may be able to use a computer free at your local library. Many public libraries let you use computers to explore the Web, use software, and send e-mail. Try to go when the library is not busy.

Circle your answers.

1. What is this consumer tip about?
   a. exploring the Web
   b. getting free computer time

2. Which sentence states the writer's point?
   a. More people should own computers.
   b. You may be able to use a computer free at your local library.

Use It

As you read this part of a science book, look for the writer's point.

Common and Scientific Names

Every animal has a common name. This is the name that most people use. But common names change from place to place, so a dog in England is a *perro* in Spain. Scientists have to be sure what animals they're talking about. So they give each animal a scientific name in Latin. The name for a dog is *Canis familiaris*. Scientists everywhere use this name. It doesn't change from place to place.

Circle your answers.

1. What is this part of the book about?
   a. habits of animals
   b. names for animals

2. Which sentence states the writer's point?
   a. Every animal has two kinds of name.
   b. Dogs have many names around the world.

Using the Writer's Point

◆ *Building on the Main Idea*

First, decide what the writer's point is. (See Lesson 10.) Keep the writer's point in mind as you read.
You may be able to figure out things that the writer never actually states.

This Is the Idea

Read this financial advice and think about the writer's point.

Pay Yourself First

Many people save only if they have money left at the end of a week. This savings plan doesn't work well, because money is seldom left over. A better way to save is to pay yourself first. Put a small sum into savings each payday. Chances are you'll never miss it, and over time it will add up.

The writer states that paying yourself first is a better way to save money. Based on this point, you can figure out why it's better. Think about what's wrong with the other way and why the writer's way is better. If you pay yourself first, the money won't be gone before you can save it.

Take a Closer Look

Read this article and think about the writer's point.

As you read, ask yourself

- What is important about the writer's point?

- Based on the writer's point, what else makes sense?

Who Needs Knots?

Years ago, many people used rope and knots in building, in toolmaking, and at sea. As time went by, rope and knots were used less and less, but many people still took pride in their knowledge of fancy knots. Today, few people know how to tie knots, because few people today have any need to use them.

Circle your answers.

1. Is the writer's point that knots are more or less important now?
   a. more important   b. less important

2. Based on this point, which makes more sense?
   a. We should all learn knots.   b. Few people need to learn knots.

Try It

Read these instructions, and think about the writer's point.

Important Instructions

You must send us this form if you want to keep your insurance. Be sure to fill out every section that applies to you. Attach an extra sheet of paper if you need more space. Sign and date the form at the bottom. Mail it back in the stamped envelope that we have included.

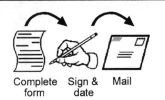

Complete form   Sign & date   Mail

Circle your answer.

1. Which sentence tells the writer's point?
    a. You must complete and mail this form to keep your insurance.
    b. You must attach an extra sheet of paper to this form.

Write your answer.

2. What might happen if you complete the form, put it in the envelope, but forget to mail it?

_____

Use It

Read this civics article, and think about the writer's point.

Could You Be President?
Americans like to say that anyone can grow up to be president. This is not actually true. The Constitution has rules about who is eligible to be president. For instance, a president must be a citizen and must have been born in the U.S. The president must also be an adult who is at least 35 years old.

Circle your answers.

1. What is the point of this text?
    a. Any American can grow up to be president.
    b. Americans don't know who can become president.
    c. There are rules about who may be president.

2. Which makes the most sense, based on the writer's point?
    a. A president might be born in Kansas.
    b. All voters must be born in this country.
    c. Some presidents will be born in Europe.

Finding Useful Details

◆ *Recognizing Significant Details*

Details are the little things in a piece of writing. Some details are more useful or important than others.
The most useful details help you understand the writer's point.

This Is the Idea

Which details are most useful in getting the point of this health tip?

STRETCHING FOR YOUR MUSCLES' SAKE

Active sports are great exercise. **Before you play, prepare your muscles by stretching.** Gentle stretching warms up cold muscles. It prepares them for movement. Stretching also helps prevent sprains and strains. Most professional athletes spend time warming up before a game.

The writer's point is in BOLD TYPE. The sentences in blue ink state important details. They help you understand the point. The first and last sentences are not as important to the point.

Take a Closer Look

As you read, ask yourself

- Is this detail useful?
- Is this a detail that I need to know to understand the writer's point?

Find the details that are most useful in taking good pictures of children.

Taking Better Pictures of Children

Pictures of children can be lively or dull, but you can take better pictures. Always have a camera with you because you never know when a child will do something cute. Take pictures with the camera low, at the child's level. Get as close to the child as possible. You don't need an expensive camera.

Check details that you need to know to take better pictures of children.

_____ a. Pictures of children can be lively or dull.

_____ b. Always have a camera with you.

_____ c. Take pictures with the camera low, at the child's level.

_____ d. You don't need an expensive camera.

Try It

Which details help you understand what a stunt pilot did?

Blanche Scott

In 1910, Blanche Scott became the first woman to fly solo, or alone. Just weeks after her first flight, she became a stunt pilot. She performed many terrifying tricks. She would dive straight toward the ground. She would fly upside down. She would fly under bridges. She thrilled audiences.

Check each detail that helps you understand what a stunt pilot did.

_____ a. Blanche Scott became the first woman to fly solo.

_____ b. She performed many terrifying tricks.

_____ c. She would fly under bridges.

_____ d. She thrilled audiences.

Use It

In this text, this is the writer's point: "Because a volcano erupted the year before, the weather was very cold in 1816."

The Year without a Summer

The year 1816 is sometimes called "The Year without a Summer." The year before that, the Tambora volcano erupted in the East Indies. Most eruptions do not affect weather. But this blast was so strong that it filled the sky with ash. Thousands of people died from the blast. In addition, the ash cut down on the warm sunlight that reached the Earth. As a result, the weather was strange that year. Snow fell in New England in June. Another cold wave struck during July. There was frost even in August.

Check each detail that helps explain the writer's point.

_____ a. Most eruptions do not affect weather.

_____ b. The blast was so strong that it filled the sky with ash.

_____ c. Thousands of people died from the blast.

_____ d. As a result, the weather was strange that year.

_____ e. There was frost even in August.

Using Details

◆ *Understanding the Significance of Details*

Some details are more useful than others. Some details help you do something. Other details help you make a choice. Look for details that tell you what you want to know.

This Is the Idea

Which details in this guide will help you visit the museum?

=== *Favorite Museums* ===

Chicago has many museums. One is the Museum of Science and Industry. This one is a favorite with children. Most love the model coal mine and the real submarine. The museum is open each day this summer from 9:30 to 5:30, except on Fridays, when it is open until 9:00 at night.

You want to know when the museum is open. The details in blue ink will help you decide when you can visit. The other details would be useful to someone else, but they don't tell you what you want to know.

Take a Closer Look

As you read, ask yourself

• What makes this detail useful?

• Will this detail help me do something or make a choice?

Which details in this chart will help you find sales of winter clothes?

CALENDAR OF SALES

MONTH	ITEMS OFTEN ON SALE
January	linens, winter clothing, small appliances
February	jewelry, winter clothing, large appliances
March	gardening items, winter clothing
April	gardening items, bicycles, luggage

Which are the best months to get winter clothes at bargain prices? Check your answers. ***Hint:*** Look for the words *winter clothing*.

_____ a. January

_____ b. February

_____ c. March

_____ d. April

Try It

Which details in this editorial will help you make your opinion known?

Make Your Opinion Known

The new tax bill has gone to the Senate. Let your senators know your ideas about this bill. Every state has two senators, who are elected for six-year terms. To find out who your senators are and how to reach them, call City Hall or look in a current almanac. If your phone book has blue pages, they also will tell you. They list government offices.

Check two details that will help you let your senator know your opinion.

_____ a. Every state has two senators.

_____ b. They are elected for six-year terms.

_____ c. Call City Hall, or look in a current almanac.

_____ d. The blue pages of a phone book will also tell you.

Use It

Which details will help you tell what kind of nest blue jays are building?

H. Stanley Johnson/SuperStock

Blue jays build courting nests and breeding nests.

Courting Nests The male blue jay takes twigs from trees and gives them to the female. She builds loose nests from these. Often these nests are flat.

Breeding Nests Both male and female gather twigs, leaves, and other objects from the ground, and both work on the nest. This nest is carefully built and often has a lining.

Circle your answers.

1. What kind of nest is flat?
   a. courting nest   b. breeding nest

2. What kind of nest has a lining?
   a. courting nest   b. breeding nest

Write your answer.

3. If a male and female jay are getting twigs, what are they building?

_____

Deciding When It Happens

◆ *Following a Sequence*

**In most reports of events, travel articles, and history articles, the events are in the same order as they happened.
In most directions, the steps are in the order that you should follow.**

This Is the Idea

As you read these directions, notice the order of the steps.

How to Make a Great Cup of Tea

Start by filling a teakettle with cold water. Put the kettle on to boil, and put loose tea leaves in a teapot. When the water boils, pour it over the leaves to fill the pot. Wait five minutes for the tea to steep. Then savor it!

These three steps are listed out of order, but are numbered to show the right order. Notice that the numbering matches the order in the text.

___3___ Pour boiling water over the tea leaves.

___1___ Put the kettle on to boil.

___2___ Put tea leaves in a teapot.

Take a Closer Look

What shows the order of events?
- the order in the text
- the words *after, again, as soon as, at last, before, first, later, second, start, then,* and *when*

Read this portion of a travel article. Notice the order of the events.

As soon as we arrived in Paris, we set out to visit the Eiffel Tower. After buying admission tickets, we took an elevator as far up as we could go. When we got out, we began climbing stairs. At last we were at the top.

Finish numbering these events to show the order in which they happened.

___1___ We arrived in Paris.

_____ We began climbing stairs.

_____ We bought admission tickets.

___5___ We were at the top.

_____ We took an elevator.

Try It

As you read this history article, notice the order of the events.

The President Who Made a Comeback

Grover Cleveland won the presidency, lost it, and won it back. The first time he ran, he won a close race. He served four years in office, and then he ran again. This time he lost in a close race, and Benjamin Harrison took office. Prices rose, and people were annoyed. In four years, Cleveland ran again, and he won—for the second time.

1. Circle the first event of the two.
   a. Cleveland lost.   b. Harrison took office.
2. Circle the first event of the two.
   a. Prices rose.   b. Harrison took office.

Use It

As you read this history article, notice the order of the events.

The Pennies That Put the Statue of Liberty Together

The story began when France gave the U.S. a statue standing for liberty. Congress agreed to the gift. The statue came to New York, but in many parts. The U.S. hadn't raised enough cash to put it up, so people began giving coins, even pennies. Before summer was over, they had given enough, and the statue was finished the next year.

Circle your answer.

1. Which was the first event of the two?
   a. Congress agreed to the gift.   b. France gave a statue.

Write your answer.

2. Number these events to show the order in which they happened.

   _____ The summer was over.

   _____ The U.S. hadn't raised enough cash.

   _____ The statue was put together.

   _____ People began giving coins, even pennies.

Using Time Order

Notice the order of steps or events and think about why they happen in that order. Think about what would happen if the order were different. Think about what is likely to happen next.

This Is the Idea

Read these directions and think about the order of steps in them.

> ### *When You've Got a Screw Loose*
>
> When wood grows old and dry, it shrinks. A screw that held a chair leg tight becomes loose, and the leg wobbles. Remove the screw. Break a wooden toothpick into short lengths and then put them into the hole. Add some wood glue. Put the screw back, and it will be tight.

The order of the steps is important. If you don't break the toothpick into short lengths before you put it in the hole, it will stick up and get in the way of the screw.

Take a Closer Look

Read this memo and think about why timing is important in it.

> ### To Our Tenants
> We will be replacing the hallway carpet next week. Please remove all personal items from the hallways before then. Please do not schedule any moves or deliveries until after the work is done.

As you read, ask yourself

- Why are the steps in this order?
- Why did the events happen in this order?
- What would happen if the order changed?
- What will probably happen next?

Circle your answers.

1. Why should you remove personal items before next week?
   a. so workers don't have to move your things to replace the carpet
   b. so your things don't make the new carpet dirty

2. What may happen if you schedule a move next week?
   a. The movers may trip on the old carpet.
   b. The movers may get in the way of workers replacing the carpet.

Try It

Read these directions and think about why timing is important.

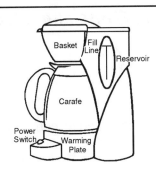

For the perfect cup of coffee—
1. Check that the power switch is set to OFF.
2. Fill the reservoir to the fill line with fresh, cold water.
3. Place a pre-measured filter pack of ground coffee in the basket.
4. Slide the basket into the holder.
5. Place the carafe on the warming plate below the basket.
6. Turn the power switch ON. This starts hot water dripping through the ground coffee.
7. When the water stops, enjoy a fresh cup of coffee.

Circle your answers.

1. What will happen if you forget to put in the filter pack before you slide the basket into the holder?
   a. The coffee will spill.
   b. The carafe will fill with hot water instead of coffee.

2. What will happen if you turn on the power switch before you put the carafe on the warming plate?
   a. The coffee will spill.
   b. The carafe will fill with hot water instead of coffee.

Use It

Read this article and think about the order of events.

The California Gold Rush

In January 1848, John Sutter was starting a ranch. Workers were building a sawmill for him on a nearby river. One of them saw a gold nugget gleaming in the water. Sutter tried to keep the gold a secret, but a man named Sam Brannan spread the word. Why? He hoped that he would make a fortune selling shovels. (He did.)

Circle your answer.

1. What did people know about Sutter's land before January 1848?
   a. He was starting a ranch there.   b. Gold had been found there.

Write your answer.

2. What did Sam Brannan hope would happen after he spread the word?

_____

Deciding Why It Happens

♦ *Recognizing Cause and Effect*

To find a cause, ask, "Why does, or did, this happen? What was the reason for it?" To find an effect, ask, "What is the result of what happened?" Look for words and patterns that signal causes and effects.

This Is the Idea

Read this advice to parents. As you do, look for causes and effects.

Putting the World in a Child's Hands

One of the best gifts you can give a child is a globe. A map is flat, but the world is round, so a map cannot show the world as it is. Because a globe is a true picture of the world, the child gets a true idea of how countries are arranged and how near or far they are.

For what reason does a map not show the world as it is? Because a map is flat and the world is round. What results from using a globe? The child gets a true idea of how countries are arranged.

Take a Closer Look

Read this business advice. As you do, look for causes and effects.

Look for

- *because:* An effect happens because a cause happens.
- *if . . . then:* If a cause happens, then an effect happens.
- *so:* A cause happens, so an effect happens.

You and Your Employees

Some people who start their own business make the mistake of not listening to their workers. Your employees do the work, so they're likely to have ideas about how to do it faster and better. If you ask them about their jobs, they will share their ideas with you.

Write your answers. The first one is done for you.

1. Why are workers likely to have ideas about how to do the work faster and better?

   <u>because they do the work</u>

2. What will result if you ask the workers about their jobs?

   _____

Try It

Read this sports advice. As you do, look for causes and effects.

When you're dressing for winter sports, you may be tempted to put on the heaviest jacket you've got. It's smarter to dress in many layers of light clothing. As you play, you'll warm up because your body is working hard. If you dress in layers, you can take a layer off when you're warm and put a layer on when you're cold.

Circle your answers.

1. Why will you warm up as you play a winter sport?
   a. because the day will get warmer
   b. because your body is working hard

2. If you dress in layers, what can you do when you're warm?
   a. take a layer off
   b. put a layer on

Use It

Read this flow chart. As you do, look for causes and effects.

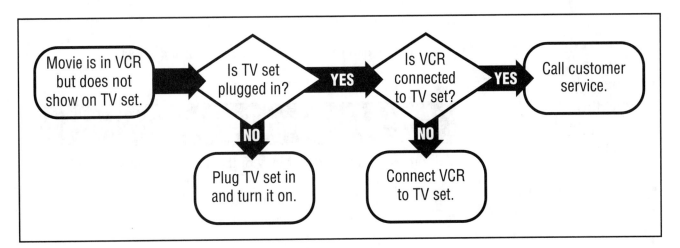

You put a movie in the VCR, but it doesn't show on the TV set. What are two things that might cause the problem? Write your answers.

1. _____

2. _____

Using Reasons

◆ *Understanding Cause and Effect*

As you read, think about why things happen. Look for causes that make something happen and effects that result from causes. Sometimes writers point out causes and effects, but sometimes you have to find them yourself.

This Is the Idea

As you read this science article, look for causes and effects.

What "Ribit" Means

The loudest frogs in the pond are male. Different types of frogs make different sounds. The noise they make is meant to attract a mate. The frog pushes air over its vocal cords to make the sound. Some have throats that fill with air to make an even louder call.

Why does a male frog make its special sound? It makes the sound to attract a mate. The writer didn't say "they make the noise because they want to attract a mate," but the words in blue ink mean the same thing.

Take a Closer Look

As you read, ask yourself

- Why did that happen?
- What made that happen?
- What caused that?
- What resulted from that?

As you read this nature article, look for causes and effects.

The Great Eel Mystery

Eels are long, skinny fish. Many of them live in freshwater streams. For a long time, people were puzzled by eels, because they never saw the babies. Then they found out that eels swim to the ocean to lay their eggs. Young eels return "home" when they're grown.

Circle your answers.

1. What caused people to be puzzled by eels?
   a. not seeing babies   b. the fact that they're skinny

2. For what reason do eels swim to the ocean?
   a. to return home   b. to lay their eggs

Try It

As you read this article, look for causes and effects.

Branches of Government

The U. S. government has three main branches that work together to run the country by its laws. The legislative branch makes the laws. The executive branch puts the laws to work. The judicial branch explains the laws. The branches check and balance each other so that none of them gets too much power.

Circle your answers.

1. Why do the three branches work together?
   a. to make the country's laws
   b. to run the country according to its laws

2. What results from the checks and balances on the branches?
   a. One branch gets much more power than the others.
   b. No one branch gets much more power than the others.

Use It

As you read this health note, look for causes and effects.

© Mitch Hrdlicka/PhotoDisc/ PictureQuest

HEALTHY BONES

Our bones get thinner as we age. For some people, mostly women, this can lead to great problems. Feeding children a balanced diet rich in calcium will help them avoid bone trouble later in life. For older people, exercise with weights can slow the thinning.

Circle your answers.

1. Why should you feed children a balanced diet rich in calcium?
   a. to make their bones thinner
   b. to help them avoid bone trouble later in life
   c. because calcium is in some foods, like milk

2. What result can older people get from exercise?
   a. The thinning of their bones will slow down.
   b. The thinning of their bones will speed up.
   c. The thinning of their bones will not change.

Finding Groups

◆ *Recognizing Classification*

Classifying is
putting things
in groups.
Writers usually
put things in
groups because
the things are alike
in some way.
Notice how they
are alike.
Think about other
things that might fit
in the group.

This Is the Idea

As you read this rate chart, notice how calling plans are grouped.

Phone Plans Compared

	Local	Long-Distance	International
Vantage	.01/min	.05/min	.09/min
CallCo	.01/min	.04/min	.10/min
NewTel	.02/min	.06/min	.08/min

The rates are grouped. If you make mostly local calls, Vantage or CallCo would be good. If you call other countries a lot, then NewTel is best.

Take a Closer Look

As you read this budget chart, notice how expenses are grouped.

Monthly Family Budget

Food	$210	Transportation	$55
Clothing	$75	Household	$45
Rent	$575	Medical	$135
Daycare	$350	Other	$55

Circle your answers. *Hint:* In each case, first think about what group the items fit in. Then check the chart to find how much is spent.

1. How much does the family plan to spend each month on coats, hats, pants, and such?
   a. $210   b. $75   c. $575

2. How much do they plan to spend on doctors, dentists, and such?
   a. $55   b. $45   c. $135

Try It

As you read this article, notice how clouds are grouped.

Meet the Heaps and Layers

There are two main families of clouds, the Heaps and the Layers. Science calls the heaps "cumulus." These are the clouds that look like heads of cauliflower. Science calls the layers "stratus." These are thin clouds that spread out in the sky. The heaps often bring rain, but the layers usually don't.

Circle your answers.

1. The kind of cloud that is more likely to bring rain
   a. looks like cauliflower.   b. spreads out in the sky.

2. The kind of cloud called cumulus
   a. looks like cauliflower.   b. spreads out in the sky.

Use It

As you read this health article, notice how foods are grouped.

▲The Food Pyramid

The food pyramid shows how to eat a balanced diet. The basic idea is that you should eat more foods from the wide bottom part of the pyramid and fewer of the foods at the narrow top.

Bread, cereal, rice, and pasta are the largest group. Two groups are just above that—vegetables and fruit. Then come two smaller groups. Milk, yogurt, and cheese is one. Meat, fish, dry beans, eggs, and nuts is the other. At the top is the smallest group: fats, oil, and sweets.

Circle your answers.

1. What group do rolls, bagels, and pita belong in?
   a. bread, cereal, rice, pasta   b. milk, yogurt, cheese

2. What group do beef, lamb, pork, and cod belong in?
   a. milk, yogurt, cheese   b. meat, fish, dry beans, eggs, nuts

Write your answer.

3. The smallest group is fats, oil, and sweets. Name one thing that fits in it.

_____

Using Groups

◆ *Understanding Classification*

This Is the Idea

Decide why the features of these apartment buildings are in groups.

	Rent	Daycare Center	Fitness Center	Laundry Center
Vista Park	$	yes	no	yes
Longview	$$	no	yes	no
Hilltop	$$$	yes	yes	yes

Each row tells about one building, and each column tells about one feature of a building. If you want to know about one building, such as the Longview, you can read across one row. If you want to compare a feature, such as a daycare center, you can read down one column.

Take a Closer Look

Read this part of an employee guide. Why does it put people in groups?

Who is eligible for the health plan?

Full-time employees are eligible after they have worked for the company for two months. Part-time employees are eligible after four months on the job.

As you read, ask yourself

- Why did the writer put things in groups?
- What do the groups mean to me?

Circle your answers. *Hint:* Decide which group you would belong in.

1. If you started working two hours a day last week, are you eligible for the health plan?

   a. yes   b. no

2. If you started working full-time a year ago, are you eligible for the health plan?

   a. yes   b. no

Try It

Read this fitness chart. Why does it put kinds of activity in groups?

Activity Type	Calories per Hour
Light (standing, ironing)	95
Medium (cleaning, vacuuming)	240
Active (raking leaves, washing car)	370
Very Active (shoveling snow, running)	580

Circle your answers.

1. How many calories will you use standing in a movie line for an hour?
   a. 95   b. 240   c. 370   d. 580

2. How many calories will you use if you spend an hour washing two small trucks?
   a. 95   b. 240   c. 370   d. 580

Use It

Read this chart from a news report and think about the groups in it.

River City Election Analysis

	Brock	Muñoz	Singer
Voters under 35	42%	34%	24%
Voters 35–50	61%	28%	11%
Voters over 50	49%	30%	21%
Men	42%	40%	18%
Women	54%	23%	23%

Circle your answers.

1. Which group supported Brock most strongly?
   a. voters under 35   b. voters 35–50   c. women

2. Which group supported Muñoz most strongly?
   a. voters over 50   b. men   c. voters under 35

Write your answer.

3. Which group supported Singer most strongly?

_____

Finding Like and Unlike

◆ *Recognizing Comparison and Contrast*

A writer may compare things. That is, the writer may tell how things are alike. A writer may contrast things. That is, the writer may tell how things are different.

This Is the Idea

Read this news item. How are the two restaurants alike and different?

Two New Restaurants

Two new restaurants opened downtown this week. The Blue Moon and Dan's Place both serve lunch and dinner. Dan's Place is lively and casual and has a special menu for children. The Blue Moon is stylish and quiet and seems like just the place for a romantic dinner for two.

How are the two restaurants alike? The text in black ink tells you that both are new, are downtown, and serve lunch and dinner. The text in blue ink explains how they are different in style and atmosphere.

Take a Closer Look

These show that things are alike:

- the same words used to describe the things
- the words *also, both, like,* and *same*

Read this graph. Decide how the budget items are alike and different.

A Look at the City Budget

Departments: Schools, Police, Fire, Parks

Budget Amount (in millions): $0 $5 $10 $15 $20 $25 $30

1. Circle a way that schools and police are alike in the budget.
   a. Both get more money than the fire or parks departments.
   b. Both get the same amount of money.

2. Circle a way that the fire and parks departments are different in the budget.
   a. Both get less money than the schools and police department.
   b. One gets more money than the other.

Try It

Read this ad. How are the old and new theaters alike and different?

> # Come See the New Windsor Theater
>
> You're in for a surprise if you haven't visited the Windsor Theater lately, because we've remodeled. Our lobby is now bigger and brighter. Our seats are wider, and they give you more legroom than the old ones. And one thing hasn't changed. Our staff is just as friendly as always.

These show that things are different:

- different words used to describe the things
- words that end in *er*, such as *wider* and *brighter*
- the words *but, however, in contrast, though, while,* and *unlike*

1. Circle one thing about the theater that is the same as it was.
   a. the name   b. the lobby

2. Circle one thing that is different now from what it was.
   a. the seats   b. the staff's friendliness

Use It

Read these two ads. How are the credit cards alike and different?

> ## ～ VISTA CARD ～
>
> You'll love the convenience of the Vista Card. Our regular interest rate is 18 percent, but if you apply now, your rate will be just 9 percent. As soon as you get your card, your credit limit will be $2,000. The Vista Card is accepted worldwide. Every charge you make earns you airline miles.

> ## Sunrise Card
>
> The Sunrise Card is getting more popular every day. Apply now, and you'll get our new member rate of 9 percent. We'll give you a starting credit limit of $1,000. You'll be able to use your Sunrise Card all over the U.S. and Canada. And you'll get airline miles every time you make a purchase.

1. Check the two that tell how the Vista and Sunrise cards are alike.

   _____ a. Your interest rate would be the same with either one.

   _____ b. Your credit limit would be the same with either one.

   _____ c. You would earn airline miles with either one.

2. Check the two that tell how the Vista and Sunrise cards are different.

   _____ a. Your interest rate would be different.

   _____ b. Your credit limit would be different.

   _____ c. You can use one in more countries than the other.

Using What You Find

◆ *Understanding Comparison and Contrast*

Look for statements that compare and contrast things. (See Lesson 20.) Use what you find to get a general idea about the things that are compared and to decide what action to take.

This Is the Idea

Why are likenesses and differences important in this book review?

TWO BOOKS FOR DOG LOVERS

World Dogs gives us a look at dogs from every country of the world. It looks at the most popular breeds in each country. *Dogs through the Ages* takes a different approach. It looks at dogs in history. It shows how dogs and people learned to get along. It shows how they learned to work together.

The review describes two books about dogs. Both sound good. Suppose you were going to buy a book for someone who loves dogs. How would you make a choice between the two books?

Take a Closer Look

Read more of the book review. Why are differences important?

World Dogs is loaded with pictures and would be ideal for a child or someone who is just getting interested in dogs. *Dogs through the Ages* would be great for the serious dog lover or breeder. Its lengthy text traces the history of dogs in human company, not only as pets, but as workers.

Think about

- what makes things alike
- what makes them different
- what you can say about the likenesses and differences in general
- why the likenesses and differences are important

Circle your answers. *Hint:* Notice the sentences in blue ink.

1. Delia just got her first puppy. Which book would you give her?
   a. *World Dogs*   b. *Dogs through the Ages*

2. Kaz raises and sells dogs. Which book would you give him?
   a. *World Dogs*   b. *Dogs through the Ages*

3. In general, which book would probably be easier to read?
   a. *World Dogs*   b. *Dogs through the Ages*

Try It

Read this subway card. Why are differences important?

Choose Your Subway Card

THE 10-RIDE CARD	THE MONTHLY CARD
10 rides plus 1 bonus ride	unlimited rides for a month
$15	$30
Anyone can use it.	Only you can use it.

Write your answers.

1. Which card would be better if you ride the subway every day?

   _____

2. Which card would be better for you and your child to share?

   _____

Use It

Why are likenesses and differences important in this nature article?

Facts about Fronts

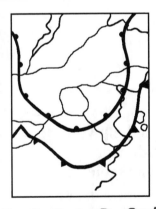

You're likely to hear about fronts when you listen to a weather forecast. A front is an imaginary line between warmer and colder air masses. A cold front means that colder air is coming. The air doesn't have to be very cold. It's colder than the air that's on its way out. A warm front means that warmer air is coming. Again, the air doesn't have to be hot. It's warmer than the air that's on the way out. One thing that both fronts have in common is the fact that they bring unsettled weather, and often bring storms.

Write your answers.

1. What is one thing that a warm front does that a cold front doesn't?

   _____

2. What is one thing that cold fronts and warm fronts both do?

   _____

Guessing What Will Happen

As you read, think about what is likely to happen as time passes. Predict what will happen. Look for hints that the writer may give you.

This Is the Idea

Read this article to predict what will happen if you observe a black bear.

> ## The Long Winter's Nap
>
> Some animals, such as ground squirrels and black bears, hibernate. That is, they spend most of the winter asleep. As winter arrives, the ground squirrel slips into a hole in the ground, curls up, and sleeps. While it sleeps, its heart works so slowly that it needs no food. When spring comes, the ground squirrel awakes and very quickly gets back to normal.

The point is that some animals, such as ground squirrels and black bears, hibernate. You can predict that when winter arrives, the black bear will go to sleep. You can predict that in spring the black bear will awake.

Take a Closer Look

Read this recipe to predict what will happen as you cook rice.

These help you decide what will happen:

- what you know
- what the writer says will happen
- a pattern of events
- the writer's point
- causes and effects
- the writer's conclusions

> ## - *Rice as You Like It* -
>
> Some like rice soft and fluffy, and others like it firmer. The secret is in the water. For one cup of long-grain white rice, use 2 cups of water if you want it fluffy and $1^3/_4$ cups if you want it firmer. Bring the water to a boil, then add the rice and stir it just once. Cover and cook over low heat until the rice has absorbed the water (15 minutes or more).

If you cook a cup of rice in 2 cups of water, how will it turn out? Circle your answer. ***Hint:*** Notice the sentence in blue ink.

    a. soft and fluffy   b. firmer   c. sticky

Try It

Read this parenting advice to predict what will happen in the morning.

End School-Morning Madness

You know what it's like when the kids are rushing off to school and can't find their homework—or their socks. To avoid mornings like that, start the night before. Have kids put their homework in a spot beside the door, always the same spot. Have them lay out their clothes. The morning will be smoother.

Circle the statement that tells what a child will find in the morning if you follow the writer's advice.

    a. The child won't know where the homework is or what to wear.

    b. The child will know where everything is and can dress quickly.

Use It

Read this consumer advice to predict what will happen to your money.

VERY INTERESTING

If you borrow money from a bank, you pay interest. If you save money in a bank, you get interest. When you use a credit card, you are borrowing money, so the bank that gave you the card charges interest. The longer you take to pay the bill, the more interest you will have to pay. On the other hand, the longer your savings stay in a bank, the more interest you will get.

Circle your answer.

1. Which statement tells what will happen if you leave your savings in a bank for a long time?
   a. You will have more money than you did at the start.
   b. You will have less money than you did at the start.

Write your answer.

2. If you wait a long time to pay a credit card bill, you will have to pay more money. Why?

_____

Using Your Prediction

◆ *Applying Predictions of Outcome*

A prediction is a good guess about what may happen as time passes. (See Lesson 22.) Use a prediction to check your understanding, to plan what you should do, and to test what the writer says.

This Is the Idea

Read this part of a driver's guide and think about what you should do.

Getting onto an Expressway_____

As you go along the approach ramp, look to the left and notice the oncoming traffic. If there is an opening, begin your entry. If not, wait until there is. As you move into the merging lane, put your left turn signal on to help the drivers behind you see that you are entering the stream of traffic.

You read the advice, and you make some guesses about what may happen in certain cases. For instance, you predict that not using your turn signal will make your car harder to see. Your prediction helps you see that this advice is meant to make getting onto an expressway safer.

Take a Closer Look

Read this part of a driver's guide and think about what you should do.

You may want to
- stop something from happening
- make sure that something does happen

Leaving an Expressway_____

Think ahead. Be aware of your exit before you reach it. Well in advance, put your right turn signal on to tell drivers behind you that you will be changing lanes and leaving the stream of traffic. Look to the right to find an opening in the traffic. Change lanes only when you have an opening.

Circle your answer. What may happen if you start to change lanes before putting your turn signal on? *Hint:* Think about the drivers behind you.

    a. Drivers behind you won't know to stay out of your way.
    b. Drivers will hold back so that they are not in your way.

Try It

Read this plant guide and think about what will happen after each step.

How to Water a Plant While You're Not There

At last you've got a chance for a vacation. What will happen to your favorite plant? To keep that plant happy, fill an empty bottle with water. Cut a length of light rope or heavy string about two feet long. Put one end in the bottle and the other in the plant's soil. Water will creep up the cord to the soil.

Circle your answer.

1. What will happen if you leave a plant without water?
   a. It will be just fine.   b. It will dry up, wither, and possibly die.

Write your answer.

2. What will happen after the water creeps all the way up the cord to the soil?

_____

Use It

Read about this form and think about what will happen after you mail it.

To Complete This Form

You must complete all items except number 7, which is optional. This application must be signed and dated in ink. If your mailing address is different from your home address, you must include both. You must mail this form no later than 25 days before the election in which you want to vote.

Mail Form						
Su	M	Tu	W	Th	F	Sa

Oct.
Nov.
Election Day

Check the *true* statements.

_____ a. If you sign the form with a pencil, you will *not* be allowed to vote.

_____ b. If you complete every item but number 7, you will *not* be allowed to vote.

_____ c. If you complete the whole form just right and mail it two weeks before the election, you will *not* be allowed to vote.

Thinking Clearly

◆ *Drawing Conclusions*

This Is the Idea

Read this article. What can you conclude about electric and gas stoves?

Cooking with Gas or Electricity

Some people like to cook with gas, and others like an electric stove. A gas stove can heat up more quickly than an electric one can. The gas stove can be cooled more quickly, too. Electric stoves are somewhat safer since there is no risk of explosion. Costs vary from place to place.

The article shows some ways that gas and electric stoves are alike and different. You can conclude that an electric stove takes longer to heat up or cool down. You can also conclude that there is some risk of explosion with gas.

Take a Closer Look

Read this article. What can you conclude about keeping warm?

Close the Gaps

Do you have gaps around the windows in your home? If you do, you might as well have a hole in the wall. You can close those gaps with caulk, foam, or even tape. Whatever you use will close the gaps at least somewhat. Closing those gaps will reduce heat loss.

Circle your answer. *Hint:* There must be a reason for what happens. Which reason explains why closing gaps will reduce heat loss? You can conclude that

a. caulk is the best way to close the gaps around windows.
b. the heat in your home can escape through small gaps.
c. foam won't close gaps well enough.

Remember
- What is true for a group is true for any thing in the group.
- If X is bigger than Y, then Y is smaller than X.
- If something happens, there must be a reason.

Try It

Read this article. What can you conclude about all bivalves?

Meet the Bivalve Family

The bivalves include clams, scallops, oysters, and mussels. Bivalves have shells with two parts joined by a hinge. Strong muscles can pull the two parts closed. The animal can hide inside, safe in its shell. The shells of bivalves come in many shapes and colors. Some are prized by collectors. In general, the scallop has a shell with ridges running out from the hinge. The clam's shell has ridges that match its oval shape.

Getty images

Circle your answers.

1. You can conclude that scallops and clams
   a. have shells with two parts joined by a hinge.
   b. have shells with ridges running outward from the hinge.

2. You can conclude that scallops
   a. have shells with ridges that match their nearly oval shape.
   b. have powerful muscles that can pull the shells closed.

Use It

Read more of the article. What can you conclude about bivalves and dinosaurs?

Those Amazing Bivalves

Bivalves are among the oldest creatures on earth. Dinosaurs appeared on Earth around 225 million years ago. By then, bivalves had been here for 300 million years. The dinosaurs are gone, but the bivalves are still here.

Getty images

1. Which were on Earth first, dinosaurs or bivalves? Write your answer.

_____

2. Creatures that no longer exist are called *extinct*. Which are extinct, dinosaurs or bivalves? Write your answer.

_____

Using Clear Thinking

◆ *Applying Conclusions*

Decide what you can conclude from what you read. (See Lesson 24.) Use what you conclude to decide what you should do, to test your understanding, and to see whether the writer's point makes sense.

This Is the Idea

Read this consumer guide. What can you conclude about the main point?

████ FASTER IS BETTER ████

It's best to pay a credit card balance as fast as you can. Let's say that your balance is $500. Your card charges 13% annual interest. In most cases, if you don't charge any more and pay $25 a month, you'll pay more than $66 in interest, but if you pay $50 a month, you'll pay only about $32 in total interest.

You can conclude that making a larger payment will save money and that making smaller payments will cost money. You'll pay more in total interest. Based on your conclusions, you may decide to pay a bill quickly and save money.

Take a Closer Look

Read this part of a review. What can you conclude about the rumors?

The Return of Elrod Grange

Last night, singer Elrod Grange gave his first public performance in two years. There had been rumors that Grange had retired and would never perform again. There were rumors that he had left the country and would not return. There were even rumors that he had died.

Circle your answer. Which of the following statements do you conclude makes more sense? *Hint:* Test each statement to see if it fits the facts.

    a. It would be best not to believe rumors about Elrod Grange.

    b. The things people say about Elrod Grange are probably true.

Try It

Read this article. What can you conclude about the stars and stripes?

THE STARS AND STRIPES

On June 14, 1777, Congress declared that the flag of the United States would have 13 stripes, red and white, with 13 white stars on a blue field. The stripes stand for the 13 colonies that first became the United States of America. Each of the stars stands for a state, and a new star was added for each new state, so today there are 50 stars.

Circle your answers.

1. From what the stripes stand for, you can conclude that
   a. there will be more stars someday.
   b. there will always be just 13 stripes.

2. From what the stars stand for, you can conclude that
   a. there are 13 states today.
   b. there are 50 states today.

Use It

Read about snakes. What can you conclude?

Snakes

There are about 2,400 different kinds of snake. The smallest may be as small as a worm when grown, but the largest can be longer than 30 feet. A snake's skin is covered with scales, like the skin of a fish. As they grow, snakes shed their skin. All snakes are meat-eaters. Depending on their size and what is available, they may eat insects, frogs, or mice.

Circle your answers.

1. An anaconda can be more than 30 feet long. What can you conclude?
   a. It is one of the largest snakes.
   b. Many snakes grow larger than the anaconda.

2. An adult Braminy blind snake is 6 inches long. What can you conclude?
   a. It probably eats mice.
   b. It probably eats insects.

Filling Gaps

◆ *Making Inferences*

Sometimes writers leave things out. They may leave out important points, even the main point. As you read, make good guesses about what's missing. In your mind, fill any gaps the writer may have left.

This Is the Idea

Read this buying guide and think about the writer's main point.

Which Life Insurance Is Right for You?

Term insurance covers the buyer for a certain term of years, not for the buyer's entire life. Many people buy it while they are young. Term life insurance costs less when the buyer is young. Whole life insurance costs a buyer more at first, but the annual payments never change.

From two statements that the writer makes, you can make a good guess about a third statement that is missing. The statements are in blue ink. From them, you can infer that payments for term insurance *do* change. They go up as a person gets older.

Take a Closer Look

As you read, ask yourself

- Are there ideas that are not clearly connected?
- Can I connect them in ways that make sense?

Read this article about a word and think about the writer's point.

DON'T PANIC!

The word *panic* names a feeling of great fear, especially if many people feel it at once. The ancient Greeks had a god named Pan. He had the body of a man and the legs, hoofs, and horns of a goat. He lived in woods and forests. At night, when travelers were making their way through the dark woods, Pan liked to make strange noises.

Which of these is a good guess about the word *panic?* Check it. **Hint:** How can you connect the meaning of *panic* with the story of Pan?

_____ a. The word *panic* comes from the way Pan pleased people.

_____ b. The word *panic* comes from the way Pan scared people.

Try It

Read this household tip and think about the writer's point.

• Storing Canned Goods •

You can safely store most canned goods for a year or more. Canned meats and poultry may be stored for 18 months, and canned fish for up to a year. Most fruits and vegetables can also be stored that long, but don't store canned citrus fruits or berries longer than six months.

1. The writer says "you can safely store most canned goods for a year or more." Circle the statement that is a good guess.
   a. Canning meat is easier than canning fish.
   b. Canned fish may become unsafe if it gets too old.

2. Circle the statement that is a good guess about the overall point of the household tip.
   a. No canned food can be stored safely forever.
   b. Canned foods are safer than frozen foods.

Use It

As you read this history article, think about the writer's point.

Cutting Logs into Boards, 1800s Style

The early sawyers worked in pairs, and they used large handsaws. First, they rolled the log over a deep pit. Then one sawyer got into the pit, while the other stood above it. They used long saws, called whipsaws, to cut the log. The man in the pit pulled down on the saw to cut the log, and the man on top pulled the saw up again after each stroke. It took the pair a long time to cut one log into boards.

Two of these statements are good guesses about logging. Check them.

_____ a. A person who saws logs is called a sawyer.

_____ b. Sawing logs was once an easy way to earn money.

_____ c. Whipsaws cut only during the upward stroke.

_____ d. A whipsaw had a handle at each end.

Using Good Guesses

**An inference is a good guess about something the writer suggested but did not say. (See Lesson 26.) You can use inferences to learn more than the writer says.
You can also use them to plan what you should do.**

This Is the Idea

Read this part of a science article, and think about the main point.

RODENTS

Rodents are a type of mammal. You can identify them by their teeth. Their front teeth never stop growing, so these mammals must gnaw on things to keep their teeth short. Most people know that mice and beavers are rodents. They chew on wood to keep their teeth short, as do squirrels.

The main point is that rodents have teeth that need special care. The writer names two kinds of rodent, mice and beavers. You can use an inference—a good guess—to decide that a squirrel is a rodent, too. You can also use inference to figure out the meaning of *gnaw* ("chew").

Take a Closer Look

As you read, ask yourself
- Do some ideas suggest other ideas?
- How can I use those new ideas?

Read this part of an art book, and think about the writer's point.

The New Artists: The Impressionists

Their paintings did not look like older ones. The new artists did not make objects look realistic. Instead, they painted to create an effect. Many focused on light and shadow. Some, including Degas, painted images of people. Others, including Monet, liked the play of light on plants and landscapes.

Circle your answers.

1. Which of these is a good guess about Monet?
   a. He was one of the earlier artists.
   b. He was one of the new artists.

2. What can you learn about Monet's style through inference?
   a. He tried to make objects look realistic.
   b. He painted to create an effect.

Try It

Read this science article and think about the writer's point.

Vitamin C

For years, sailors knew that limes protected them from a disease called scurvy. The vitamin C in the limes kept the sailors safe. Limes are not the only good source of this vitamin. Oranges, lemons, and grapefruit have it, too. Even green peppers can ward off scurvy, if you eat enough of them.

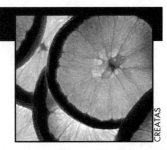

Circle your answer.

1. Which sentence is a good guess at the writer's point?
   a. Sea air causes scurvy.
   b. Vitamin C prevents scurvy.

Write a useful inference.

2. Eating fruits and vegetables _____

_____ .

Use It

Read this article about weather and think about the writer's point.

Storm Brings Hail

This last storm brought high winds, rain, and hail. The hail was small and melted quickly. A few hailstones have been large enough to cause damage and even death. In 1978, a bad storm struck Montana. Some of its hailstones were as big as baseballs. Hundreds of sheep were killed in the storm.

Circle your answers.

1. Which is a good guess about the last hailstorm?
   a. It probably caused a lot of damage.
   b. It probably caused very little damage.

2. Which is a useful inference?
   a. The year 1978 was cold in Montana.
   b. It's a good idea to seek cover during a bad hailstorm.

Getting the Big Picture

◆ *Making Generalizations*

As you read, pause now and then to step back from the details.
Think about the general meaning of the text.
If you can, write a general statement about the facts and ideas in the text.

This Is the Idea

Read this article. What can you say in general about the foods in it?

Nuts or Not Nuts?

If you go to a market, you'll find a wide selection of nuts. There will be almonds, peanuts, and hazelnuts. From a scientist's point of view, only the last of those is a nut. Almonds are pits, like peach pits or olive pits. Peanuts are seeds in pods, much more like peas than nuts.

The article points out that we call almonds and peanuts nuts. But scientists would not call them nuts. You could say, in general, that some of the foods we call nuts are not nuts from science's point of view.

Take a Closer Look

Ask yourself
• What is the general idea?

Look at this graph. What can you say in general about all the cities?

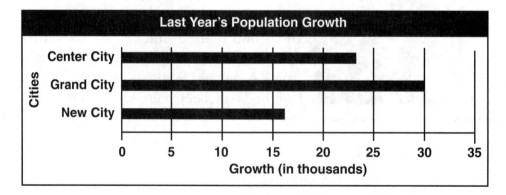

Which is the best general statement about the graph? Circle your answer.
Hint: Your statement has to be true of all the cities.
a. These cities all grew by 15,000 people or more.
b. Grand City grew faster than New City.
c. New City grew more slowly than Center City did.

Try It

What can you say in general about the vegetables in this article?

The Leafy Greens

In any supermarket, you'll find fresh, leafy green vegetables. Lettuce and spinach are high in calcium. If you don't like those, try bok choy, which is sometimes called Chinese cabbage. It's high in calcium, too. So are turnip greens.

Which general statement is better? Circle your answer.

   a. Many leafy green vegetables are a great source of calcium.

   b. Spinach and bok choy are great sources of calcium.

Use It

Look at this graph. What can you say in general about the month?

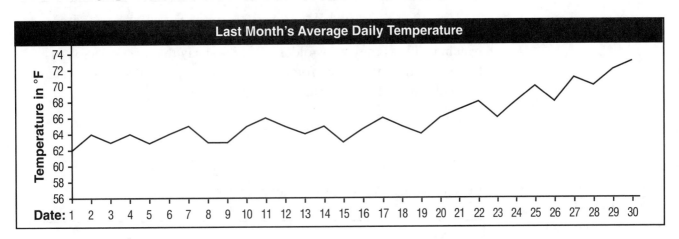

Circle your answers.

1. Did the temperature go up every day?

   a. yes   b. no

2. In general, does the line on the graph go up or down from the 1st to the 30th?

   a. up   b. down

Write your answer.

3. What general statement can you make about the temperature this month?

_____

Checking the Big Picture

◆ *Testing Generalizations*

As you read, pause now and then to make a general statement about the facts and ideas in the text. (See Lesson 28.) **Look for general statements that the writer makes, too.**

This Is the Idea

Look at this graph. It shows how much time people in River City spend watching TV. What can you say in general about it?

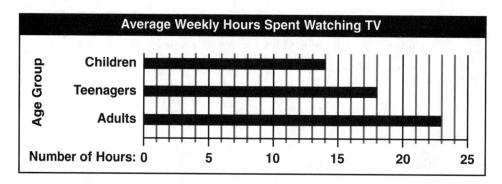

You could say, in general, that people in River City spend more time watching TV as they grow older. Could you say that *every* person in River City does that? No. You can only make a general statement. The graph doesn't tell you about individual people.

Take a Closer Look

Ask yourself

- Does the general statement fit the facts?
- Does it cover all the facts?
- Does it make sense or does it go too far?
- Is it fair?

Read this note. What can you say in general about it?

Dear Gamal,

We arrived in Nashville Tuesday morning, during heavy rain. Wednesday was also rainy, so we didn't see much. On Thursday, the rain was light, so we did some sightseeing, but today the heavy rain returned, and this is my last day here!

Nera

Which general statement fits the facts and is fair? Circle your answer.
Hint: Which statement goes beyond the facts? That one isn't fair.
a. It rained throughout Nera's stay in Nashville.
b. It always rains in Nashville.

Try It

Think about the writer's general statements in this sports column.

Lizards Win Again

The River City Lizards are off to a great start this year. They've won their first 10 games, holding opposing teams to two runs in every game. They lead the league in hitting, with three players in the top 10. This team can't lose.

Circle your answers.

1. What will the River City Lizards do as the year goes by?
   a. They will play more games.
   b. They won't play any more games.

2. The writer makes two general statements. Which one makes sense?
   a. The River City Lizards are off to a great start this year.
   b. This team can't lose.

Use It

Think about the writer's general statements in this travel article.

Dining in Australia

Getty images

On a restaurant menu, I found "witchity grubs." When I asked what they were, I was told that they are an insect. The waitress assured me that they were "very tasty." On other menus, I saw kangaroo listed. I saw several people eating these things, and they all assured me that they were "very tasty." It seems to me that Australians will eat anything that crawls or hops.

Circle your answers.

1. The writer says that "Australians will eat anything that crawls or hops." What is wrong with that general statement?
   a. It doesn't fit the facts.
   b. It goes too far.

2. Which of these would be a better general statement?
   a. Some people will eat things that I wouldn't.
   b. Australians will eat anything.

Finding the Facts

♦ *Separating Fact from Opinion*

A fact is true and can be proved.
An opinion is what someone feels or believes.
An opinion cannot be proved, since different people have different feelings and beliefs, but facts are the same for everyone.

This Is the Idea

Which parts of this ad for a used car are statements of fact?

Varona Sedan for Sale

This car is a great bargain! It is two years old and has been driven 22,000 miles. This car has everything anyone could possibly want. It has power windows and locks, and it has a tape deck by BellArte that was voted best by *Car 'n' Music* magazine. Anyone would be proud to drive this car.

You could prove the statements in blue ink. You could look at the car and check the model, miles, and equipment. At a library, you could check the detail about the sound system. You could prove these statements.

You can't prove the statements in black ink. Those are the writer's opinions. You may agree, or you may not.

Take a Closer Look

Which parts of this profile are statements of fact?

Dorothea Lange

Lange began working as a photographer in the 1920s. At that time, she made portraits of rich people. Those pictures don't interest us now. In the 1930s, she began taking pictures of poor people, including portraits of farm workers, their children, and people out of work. Those pictures will tug at your heart.

Here are ways that you can check statements of fact:

- You can observe—see with your own eyes—that it is true.
- You can check it in a reliable source.

1. Draw lines under the statements of fact. **Hints:** Read each sentence. Could you prove it by checking a good source?

2. Draw lines through the two statements that are not facts. **Hint:** Look for statements that tell how the writer feels about the pictures.

Try It

Which parts of this safety tip are statements of fact?

Read That Label!

Many people don't read the labels on their pills. These labels contain a great deal of information. They tell what drugs are in the pills and the dosage for adults and children. They also tell how to store the pills. Labels contain warnings that can save lives. Everyone should read them.

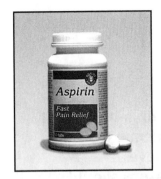

Put a check mark in front of each statement of fact. Remember: you can prove that a statement of fact is true or you can test it.

_____ a. These labels contain a great deal of information.

_____ b. They tell what drugs are in the pills and how to store them.

_____ c. Labels contain warnings that can save lives.

_____ d. Everyone should read them.

Use It

Which parts of this editorial are opinions?

Teen Center

Money for a teen center has been cut from the budget again. This is a disgrace. This center would be a place where young people could spend their after-school hours. The planned center would be open daily. It would provide study rooms, computers, and sports facilities. Our city needs a place like this.

The editorial contains two statements of opinion. What are they? Write your answers. *Hint:* An opinion tells what someone feels or believes.

1. _____

2. _____

Thinking about Opinions

◆ *Evaluating Opinions*

An opinion is what someone feels or believes.
Reasons should support opinions.
Facts should back them up.
Look for reasons and facts when you judge an opinion.

This Is the Idea

Look for facts and opinions in this notice.

———— **Paper or Plastic?** ————

From now on, our store will use paper bags unless you ask for plastic. This is a change in our policy. We used to ask which type of bag you wanted. We now believe that paper is a better choice. People can recycle paper. Also, plastic does not break down in the ground, while paper does.

There is just one opinion in this notice, and the writer tells you that it is an opinion. It is shown in blue. Everything in black ink is a statement of fact. Are these all the facts you need to judge the opinion?

Take a Closer Look

As you read, look for opinions and ask yourself

• Does the writer support opinions with reasons and facts?

• Does the writer give all the facts?

Read this part of a letter, and think about the writer's opinions.

Dear Store Manager:

I received your notice about the bags. I think you should use only plastic bags. Like paper, plastic can be recycled. In fact, it can be recycled more than one time. True, plastic stays in the ground for years, but so does buried paper. Only paper on top of the ground breaks down quickly.

Write your answers. *Hints:* Look for statements that tell why plastic bags are good. Look for statements about paper as well.

1. The writer thinks _____ .

2. What is one reason or fact that the writer gives?

_____

Try It

Read this part of a letter and think about the writer's opinions.

Dear Manager:

You are not thinking clearly! Paper and plastic bags are both poor choices. They will ruin our Earth. We should avoid both kinds of bags and use cloth bags instead. One cloth bag can be used over and over again. You should sell these at your store or even give them away.

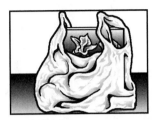

Write your answers.

1. What does this writer think of plastic and paper bags?

   _____

2. What sentence in this letter states a fact?

   _____

   _____

Use It

Read this editorial and think about the writer's opinion.

Paper or Plastic

Choosing paper or plastic is not easy. Both use up resources when they are made. Paper uses trees, water, and oil. Plastic uses oil and heating fuel. Both kinds of bags can either be thrown out or recycled. Recycling a bag is more important than the kind of bag you use.

Write your answers.

1. What facts does the writer give about paper *and* plastic bags?

   _____

   _____

2. What is the writer's opinion?

   _____

   _____

Answer Key

Lesson 1

Take a Closer Look
1. b   2. a

Try It
1. a   2. b

Use It
1. a   2. b   3. a   4. b

Lesson 2

Take a Closer Look
b

Try It
1. b   2. a

Use It
1. a   2. b   3. a

Lesson 3

Take a Closer Look
c

Try It
1. b   2. a

Use It
1. a   2. b

Lesson 4

Take a Closer Look
1. a   2. b

Try It
1. a   2. b

Use It
1. a   2. a   3. b   4. b

Lesson 5

Take a Closer Look
1. Answers will vary but should come from the first column.
2. Answers will vary but should come from the second column.

Try It
1. should be put in the first column
2. should be put in the second column
3. Answers will vary but should be put in the first column.
4. Answers will vary but should be put in the second column.

Use It
Answers will vary but should be put in the third column.

Lesson 6

Take a Closer Look
a, b

Try It
c

Use It
c

Lesson 7

Take a Closer Look
b

Try It
b

Use It
1. a   2. a

Lesson 8

Take a Closer Look
1. a   2. a

Try It
1. a   2. b   3. b

Use It
1. b   2. b   3. b

Lesson 9

Take a Closer Look
b, c

Try It
a, d

Use It
1. c   2. b

Lesson 10

Take a Closer Look
1. a   2. b

Try It
1. b   2. b

Use It
1. b   2. a

Lesson 11

Take a Closer Look
1. b   2. b

Try It
1. a
2. You might lose your insurance.

Use It
1. c   2. a

Lesson 12

Take a Closer Look
b, c

Try It
b, c, d

Use It
b, d, e

Lesson 13

Take a Closer Look
a, b, c

Try It
c, d

Use It
1. a
2. b
3. a breeding nest

Lesson 14

Take a Closer Look
1, 4, 2, 5, 3

Try It
1. a   2. b

Use It
1. b
2. 3, 1, 4, 2

Lesson 15

Take a Closer Look
1. a   2. b

Try It
1. b   2. a

Use It
1. a
2. that he would make a fortune selling shovels

Lesson 16

Take a Closer Look
2. They will share their ideas with you.

Try It
1. b   2. a

Use It
1. The TV set isn't plugged in.
2. The VCR isn't connected to the TV set.

Lesson 17

Take a Closer Look
1. a   2. b

Try It
1. b   2. b

Use It
1. b   2. a

Lesson 18

Take a Closer Look
1. b   2. c

Try It
1. a   2. a

Use It
1. a
2. b
3. Answers will vary.

Lesson 19

Take a Closer Look
1. b   2. a

Try It
1. a   2. c

Use It
1. b
2. b
3. voters under 35

Lesson 20

Take a Closer Look
1. a   2. b

Try It
1. a   2. a

Use It
1. a, c   2. b, c

Lesson 21

Take a Closer Look
1. a   2. b   3. a

Try It
1. The Monthly Card
2. The 10-Ride Card

Use It
1. It brings warmer air.
2. Answers may vary. Any of these are OK:
   They lie between warmer and colder
   air masses.
   They bring different temperature air.
   They bring unsettled weather.

Lesson 22

Take a Closer Look
a

Try It
b

Use It
1. a
2. You have to pay more interest when you
   take longer to pay your bill.

Lesson 23

Take a Closer Look
a

Try It
1. b
2. The water will moisten the soil.

Use It
a, c

Lesson 24

Take a Closer Look
b

Try It
1. a   2. b

Use It
1. bivalves
2. dinosaurs

Lesson 25

Take a Closer Look

a

Try It

1. b   2. b

Use It

1. a   2. b

Lesson 26

Take a Closer Look

b

Try It

1. b   2. a

Use It

a, d

Lesson 27

Take a Closer Look

1. b   2. b

Try It

1. b
2. protects you from the disease called scurvy

Use It

1. b   2. b

Lesson 28

Take a Closer Look

a

Try It

a

Use It

1. b
2. a
3. In general, the month got warmer.

Lesson 29

Take a Closer Look

a

Try It

1. a   2. a

Use It

1. b   2. a

Lesson 30

Take a Closer Look

1. Lange began working as a photographer in the 1920s.
   At that time, she made portraits of rich people.
   In the 1930s, she began taking pictures of poor people, including portraits of farm workers, their children, and people out of work.
2. Those pictures don't interest us now.
   Those pictures will tug at your heart.

Try It

a, b, c

Use It

a. This is a disgrace.
b. Our city needs a place like this.

Lesson 31

Take a Closer Look

1. *you should use only plastic bags*
2. Answers will vary. Any of these is OK:
   Plastic can be recycled.
   Plastic can be recycled more than one time.
   Plastic stays in the ground for years, but so does buried paper.
   Only paper on top of the ground breaks down quickly.

Try It

1. They are both poor choices.
2. One cloth bag can be used over and over again.

Use It

1. Both use up resources. Both can be thrown out or recycled.
2. Recycling a bag is more important than the kind of bag you use.